100 FACTS

ANCIENT EGYPT

100 FACTS
ANCIENT EGYPT

Jane Walker

Consultant: Richard Tames

Sandy Creek
NEW YORK

An Imprint of Sterling Publishing
387 Park Avenue South
New York, NY 10016

© 2001 by Miles Kelly Publishing Ltd.

This 2013 edition published by Sandy Creek.

Publishing Director: Belinda Gallagher
Creative Director: Jo Cowan
Editorial Assistant: Bethanie Bourne
Volume Designer: Sally Lace
Picture Researcher: Liberty Newton
Proofreader/Indexer: Lynn Bresler
Production Manager: Elizabeth Collins
Reprographics: Anthony Cambray, Jennifer Hunt
Assets: Lorraine King

ISBN 978-1-4351-5081-2

ACKNOWLEDGMENTS
The publishers would like to thank the following artists
who have contributed to this book:

Chris Buzer/Studio Galante, Vanessa Card, Mike Foster/Maltings Partnership,
Terry Gabbey/AFA, Peter Gregory, Richard Hook/Linden Artists Ltd,
John James/Temple Rogers, Janos Marffy, Roger Payne/Linden Artists Ltd,
Eric Rowe/Linden Artists Ltd, Peter Sarson, Rob Sheffield
Nick Spender/Advocate, Roger Stewart, Rudi Vizi

Mike White/Temple Rogers

Cartoons by Mark Davis at Mackerel

The publishers would like to thank the following sources for the use of their photographs:
Front cover: PhotoDiscs, back cover: Eugene Sergeev/Shutterstock.com

All other images come from Miles Kelly Archives

Every effort has been made to acknowledge the source and copyright holder of each picture.
Miles Kelly Publishing apologizes for any unintentional errors or omissions.

Made with paper from a sustainable forest

Manufactured in China
Lot #:
2   4   6   8   10   9   7   5   3   1

05/13

Contents

The heart of ancient Egypt

1 **Without the waters of the river Nile, the amazing civilization of ancient Egypt might never have existed.** The Nile provided water for drinking and for watering crops. Every year its floods left a strip of rich dark soil on both sides of the river. Farmers grew their crops in these fertile strips. The Egyptians called their country Kemet, which means "black land," after this dark soil. The Nile was also important for transport, it was a highway for the Egyptians!

Royal news

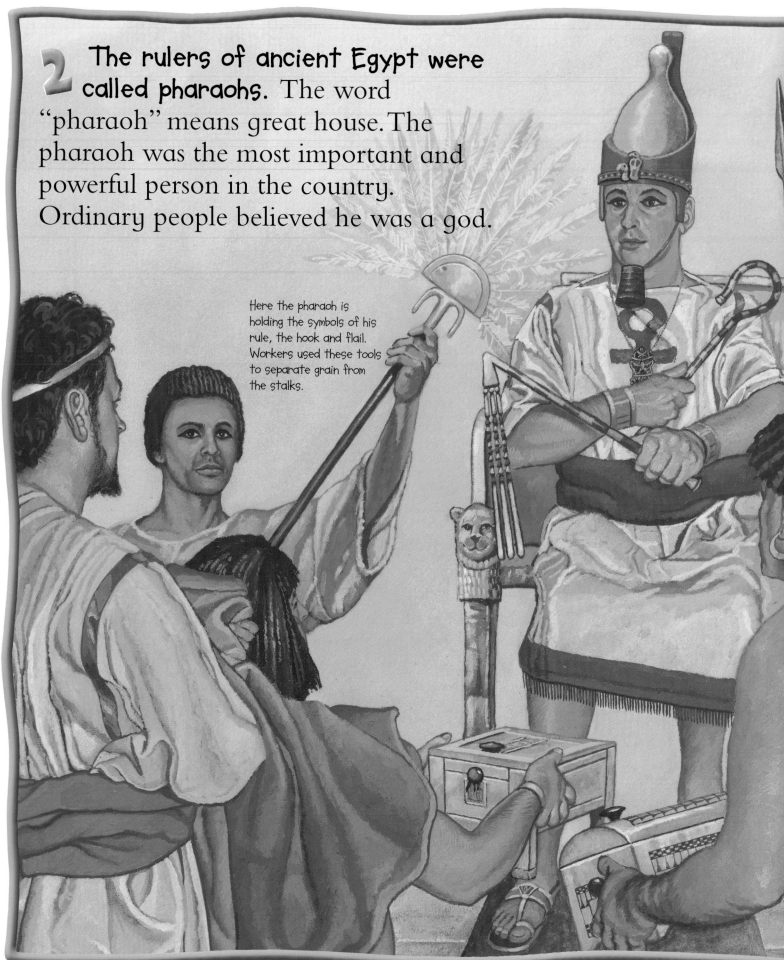

2 **The rulers of ancient Egypt were called pharaohs.** The word "pharaoh" means great house. The pharaoh was the most important and powerful person in the country. Ordinary people believed he was a god.

Here the pharaoh is holding the symbols of his rule, the hook and flail. Workers used these tools to separate grain from the stalks.

3 Ramses II ruled for over 60 years. He was the only pharaoh to carry the title "the Great" after his name. Ramses was a great builder and a brave soldier. He was also the father of an incredibly large number of children: 96 boys and 60 girls. Imagine having 156 brothers and sisters!

These people are paying tribute to the pharaoh. This means that they have come from the surrounding countries to give him presents and tell him how great he is!

4 The pharaoh often married a close female relative, such as his sister or half-sister. In this way the blood of the royal family remained pure. The title of "pharaoh" was usually passed on to the eldest son of the pharaoh's most important wife.

I DON'T BELIEVE IT!

On special occasions, women courtiers wore hair cones made of animal fat scented with spices and herbs. The melting fat trickled down their heads, making their hair sweet smelling—and greasy!

Powerful people

5 More than 30 different dynasties ruled ancient Egypt. A dynasty is a line of rulers from the same family.

6 More than 7,000 years ago, people from central Africa began to arrive in Egypt. They settled in villages along the banks of the Nile and around the Nile Delta. These villages formed the two kingdoms of Upper Egypt (Nile Valley) and Lower Egypt (Nile Delta).

Crown of Lower Egypt

Crown of Upper Egypt

▲ The double crown of Egypt was made up of two crowns, the bucket–shaped red crown of Lower Egypt and the bottle–shaped white crown of Upper Egypt.

▼ This timeline shows the dates of the dynasties of ancient Egypt. The dates are given as a yearBC. This means Before Christ. We also say AD, by which we mean After Christ. The year IAD is the date from which we start counting the years.

Egypt's first pyramid, the Step Pyramid, was built in 2650BC

**2750–2250BC
OLD KINGDOM
(Dynasties III–VI)**

The Hyksos people invaded in 1670BC and introduced the chariot

**2025–1627BC
MIDDLE KINGDOM
(Dynasties XI–XIII)**

The tomb of the New Kingdom pharaoh Tutankhamun was discovered in 1922

**1539–1070BC
NEW KINGDOM
(Dynasties XVIII–XX)**

**3100–2750BC
EARLY DYNASTIC PERIOD
(Dynasties I and II)**

King Narmer, also called Menes, unites Egypt and records his deeds on what we call the Narmer palette

**2250–2025BC
FIRST INTERMEDIATE PERIOD
(Dynasties VII–X)**

As the civilization progressed, the Egyptians introduced gods for all different areas of life

**1648–1539BC
SECOND INTERMEDIATE PERIOD
(Dynasties XIV–XVII)**

Nilometers were invented to keep track of the height of the river, which was very important for the crops

**1070–653BC
THIRD INTERMEDIATE PERIOD
(Dynasties XXI–XXV)**

The god Ra was identified at this time with Amun, and became Amun–Ra who was the king of the gods

7 **The history of ancient Egypt began more than 5,000 years ago.** The first period was called the Old Kingdom, when the Egyptians built the Great Pyramids. Next came the Middle Kingdom and finally the New Kingdom.

◀ Pharaoh Pepi II (2246–2152BC), had the longest reign in history—94 years. He became king when he was only six years old.

Queen Cleopatra was the last ruler of the Ptolemaic period.

332–30BC
PTOLEMAIC PERIOD

664–332BC
LATE PERIOD
(Dynasties
XXVI–XXXI)

In 332BC Alexander the Great conquered Egypt and founded the famous city of Alexandria.

30BC–AD395
ROMAN PERIOD

The Roman Emperor Octavian conquered Egypt in 30BC.

▲ This vizier is checking the sacks of grain that have been brought in from the harvest while a criminal awaits his punishment. The viziers of ancient Egypt were among the most important people in the country.

8 **Officials called viziers helped the pharaoh to govern Egypt.** Each ruler appointed two viziers —one each for Upper and Lower Egypt. Viziers were powerful men. Each vizier was in charge of a number of royal overseers. Each overseer was responsible for a particular area of government, for example the army or granaries where the grain was stored. The pharaoh, though, was in charge of everyone.

I DON'T BELIEVE IT!

Farmers tried to bribe tax collectors by offering them gifts of goats or ducks in exchange for a smaller tax charge.

39 Egyptians traded with a large number of countries in the Middle East and Africa. Traders brought back silver from Syria, cedar wood, oils, and horses from Lebanon, copper from Cyprus, a gem called lapis lazuli from Afghanistan, and ebony wood and ivory from central Africa.

The Egyptians traveled to the land of Punt to bring back incense. We do not know exactly where the land of Punt is today, but we know that the Egyptians thought of it as a far away and exciting place

40 When goods were sold they were weighed using a balance and special copper weights called deben. An item could be exchanged for its equivalent weight in copper. A bed, for example, had a value of 25 deben. Pieces of gold and silver were also weighed and used as payment.

The farmer's year

41 The farming year was divided into three seasons: the flood, the growing period, and the harvest. Most people worked on the land, but farmers could not work between July and November because the land was covered by flood waters. Instead, they went off to help build the pyramids and royal palaces.

42 The river Nile used to flood its banks in July each year. The flood waters left a strip of rich black soil, about 6mi (10km) wide, along each bank. Apart from these fertile strips and a few scattered oases, pools of water in the desert, the rest of the land was mainly just sand.

44 Water was lifted from the Nile using a device called a shaduf. It was a long pole with a wooden bucket hanging from a rope at one end, and a weight at the other. The pole was supported by a wooden frame. One person working alone could operate a shaduf.

Tax collectors would often decide how rich a person was by counting how many cattle he owned

43 Egyptian farmers had to water their crops because of the hot, dry climate with no rain. They dug special channels around their fields along which the waters of the Nile could flow. In this way farmers could water their crops all year round. This was called irrigation, and it is still done today.

Almost no rain fell on the dry, dusty farmland of ancient Egypt. No crops would grow properly without the water from the Nile

45

Farmers used wooden plows pulled by oxen to prepare the soil for planting. They also had wooden hoes. The seeds were mainly planted by hand. At harvest time, wooden sickles edged with stone teeth were used to cut the crops.

46

Harvesting the grain was only the start of the process.
In the threshing room people would beat the grain to separate it from the chaff, the shell, of the grain. It was then winnowed. Men would throw the grain and chaff up into the air and fan away the chaff. The heavier grain dropped straight to the floor. The grain was then gathered up and taken to the granary to be stored.

47

Wheat and barley (for bread and beer) were the two main crops grown by the ancient Egyptians. They also grew grapes (for wine) and flax (to make linen). A huge variety of fruits and vegetables grew in the fertile soil, including dates, figs, cucumbers, melons, onions, peas, leeks, and lettuces.

I DON'T BELIEVE IT!

Instead of using scarecrows, Egyptian farmers hired young boys to scare away the birds— they had to have a loud voice and a good aim with a slingshot!

Farmers had to hand over part of their harvest each year as a tax payment. It was usually given to the local temple in exchange for use of the temple's land

48

Egyptian farmers kept cattle as well as goats, sheep, ducks, and geese. Some farmers kept bees to produce honey, which was used for sweetening cakes and other foods.

Winnowers separate the grain from the chaff

Getting around

49 The main method of transport in ancient Egypt was by boat along the river Nile. The Nile is the world's longest river. It flows across the entire length of the desert lands of Egypt.

50 The earliest kinds of boat were made from papyrus reeds. They were propelled by a long pole and, later on, by oars. Gradually, wooden boats replaced the reed ones, and sails were added.

These early boats were made of bundles of reeds tied together

Alexandria • • Tanis
• Avaris
Giza • • Memphis
Saqqara •

El–Amarna •

Valley of the Kings • • Karnak
Thebes • • Luxor

• Aswan

LOWER
NUBIA

Abu Simbel •

UPPER
NUBIA

Kerma • • KUSH

Red
Sea

Blue Nile

White Nile

▲ The total length of the river Nile is around 4,135mi (6,670km). To the south of Egypt, the Nile has two main branches—the White Nile and the Blue Nile.

51 A magnificent carved boat was built to carry the body of King Khufu at his funeral. Over 140ft (42m) long, it was built from planks of cedar wood. The boat was buried in a special pit next to the Great Pyramid.

▼ The cabin on board Khufu's funerary boat was decorated with carved flowers. Other traditional designs were carved into the boat. The joints were held together with strips of leather.

Steering oars

Cabin for coffin

52 Wooden barges carried blocks of limestone across the river Nile for the pyramids and temples. The stone came from quarries on the opposite bank to the site of the pyramids. The granite used to build the insides of the pyramids came from much farther away—from quarries at Aswan 500mi (800km) upstream.

Simple wooden barges like these were essential for the building work that went on in Egypt

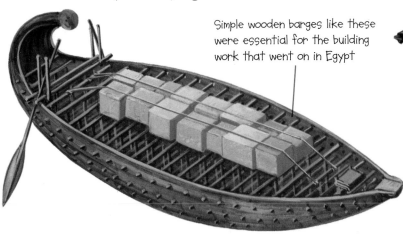

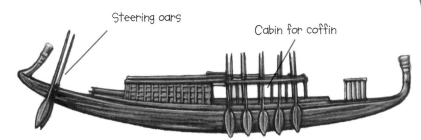

QUIZ 2

How well do you know your gods and goddesses? Can you name these:

1. This god has a jackal's head and hangs around dead bodies.

2. This god's magic eye will protect you from evil.

3. Cats are really fond of this goddess.

4. This god is a bit of a snappy character!

1.Anubis 2. Horus 3.Bastet 4. Sobek

53 Wooden-built trading ships were propelled by a combination of sail and oar power. Wide-bodied cargo boats were used to ferry cattle across the Nile. The animals stood on deck during the crossing.

Who's who?

54 The people of ancient Egypt were organized into three classes: upper, middle, and lower. The royal family, government officials, senior priests and priestesses, scribes, and doctors made up the upper class. Traders, merchants, and craftworkers were middle class. The biggest group of people by far—the unskilled workers—made up the lower class.

◀ The arrangement of Egyptian society can be shown as a pyramid shape. The pharaoh sits at the top of the pyramid, with the huge mass of unskilled laborers at the bottom.

Viziers and priests

Scribes and noblemen

Craftworkers and dancers

Carrying grain from the fields

Peasant workers winnowing grain

55 The man was the head of any Egyptian household. On his father's death, the eldest son inherited the family's land and riches. Egyptian women had rights and privileges too. They could own property and carry out businesses deals, and women from wealthy families could become doctors or priestesses.

Egypt, Old Kingdom

Egypt, Middle Kingdom

Egypt, New Kingdom

▲ These maps show the extent of the Egyptian empire in the three kingdoms.

56 Most ancient Egyptians lived along the banks of the river Nile or in the river valley. As Egypt became more powerful they spread out, up along the river Nile and around the Mediterranean Sea. Others lived by oases, pools of water in the desert.

57

Rich families had several servants, who worked as maids, cooks, and gardeners. In large houses the servants had their own quarters separate from those of the family.

▲ Family life played an important role in ancient Egypt. Couples could adopt children if they were unable to have their own.

58

Dogs and cats were the main family pets. Egyptians also kept pet monkeys and sometimes flocks of tame doves. Some people trained their pet baboons to climb fig trees and pick the ripe fruits.

59

Young children played with wooden and clay toys. Popular toys were carved animals—often with moving parts—spinning tops, toy horses, dolls, and clay balls. Children also played games which are still played today, such as leapfrog and tug-of-war.

I DON'T BELIEVE IT!

Wealthy Egyptians wanted servants in the afterlife too. They were buried with models of servants, called shabtis, that were meant to come to life and look after their dead owner!

Home sweet home

60 Egyptian houses were made from mud bricks dried in the sun. Mud was taken from the river Nile, and straw and pebbles were added to make it stronger. The trunks of palm trees supported the flat roofs. The inside walls of houses were covered with plaster, and often painted. Wealthy Egyptians lived in large houses with several stories. A poorer family, though, might live in a crowded single room.

◀ A mixture of mud, straw, and stones was poured into wooden frames or shaped into bricks and left to harden in the sun.

61 In most Egyptian homes there was a small shrine. Here, members of the family worshiped their household god.

The dwarf god, Bes, was the ancient Egyptian god of children and the home

62 Egyptians furnished their homes with wooden stools, chairs, tables, storage chests, and carved beds. A low three- or four-legged footstool was one of the most popular items of furniture. Mats of woven reeds covered the floors.

63 Rich families lived in spacious villas in the countryside. A typical villa had a pond filled with fish, a walled garden and an orchard of fruit trees.

The Egyptians used woven papyrus mats instead of carpets

64 They cooked their food in a clay oven or over an open fire.

Most kitchens were equipped with a cylinder-shaped oven made from bricks of baked clay. They burned either charcoal or wood as fuel. They cooked food in two-handled pottery saucepans.

Senet was a popular board game in ancient Egypt. Experts today think it was probably a bit like ludo

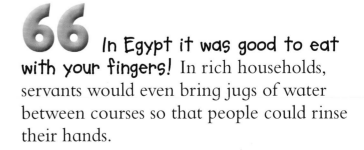

QUIZ 3

1. Why did the Egyptians bury a boat next to their pharaoh?

2. Which part of the body was left inside a mummy?

3. Who was Howard Carter?

4. Why did farmworkers have nothing to do between July and November each year?

1. So he can use it in the next life 2. The heart 3. The man who discovered the tomb of Tutankhamun 4. The river Nile had flooded the farmland

65 Pottery lamps provided the lighting in Egyptian homes.

They filled the container with oil and burned a wick made of cotton or flax. Houses had very small windows, and sometimes none at all, so there was often very little natural light. Small windows kept out the strong sunlight, helping to keep houses cool.

66 In Egypt it was good to eat with your fingers! In rich households, servants would even bring jugs of water between courses so that people could rinse their hands.

Dressing up

67 Egyptians wore lucky charms called amulets. The charms were meant to protect the wearer from evil spirits and to bring good luck. One of the most popular ones was the wadjat eye of the god Horus. Children wore amulets shaped like fish to protect them from drowning in the river Nile.

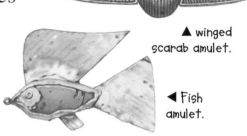

◄ The eye of Horus was thought to protect everything behind it. The god Horus had his eye torn out while defending the throne of Egypt. Later, the eye was magically repaired.

▲ winged scarab amulet.

◄ Fish amulet.

68 In Egypt, men and women both wore eye make-up. A special black eye make-up, called kohl, was made from ground-up raw metals mixed with oil. The Egyptians believed it had magical healing powers and could restore bad eyesight and fight eye infections. Egyptians also used face rouge for the cheeks and lips, face powder, paint for fingernails, and hair dyes.

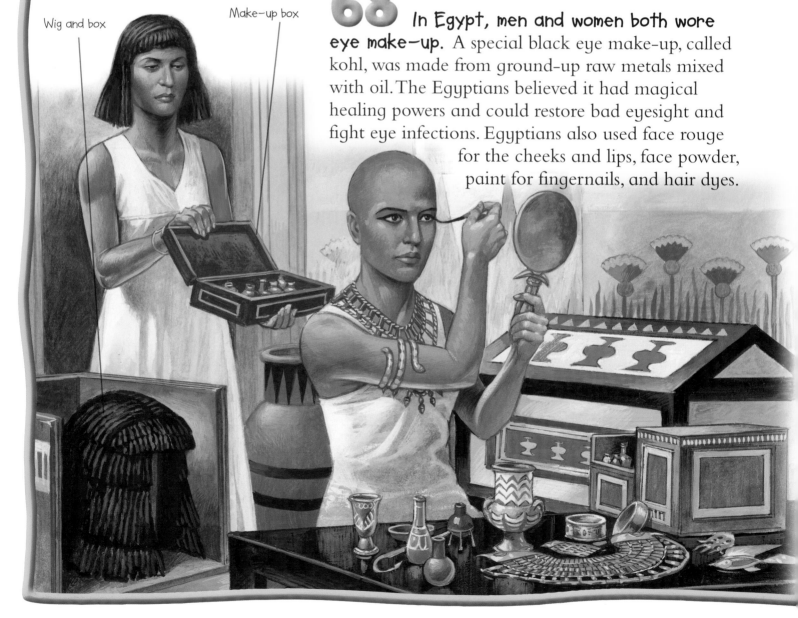

Wig and box

Make-up box

69

Most clothes were made from light-colored linen. Women wore long dresses, often with pleated cloaks. Noblewomen's dresses were made of the best cloth with beads sewn onto it. Men wore either robes or kiltlike skirts, a piece of linen wrapped around the waist and tied in a decorative knot.

▶ This fine long dress is worn with a see-through cloak. Clothes like these made sure that the people of Egypt kept cool in the hot weather.

70

Wealthy people wore wigs made from human hair or sheep's wool which they kept in special boxes on stands at home. Girls wore their hair in pigtails, while boys mostly had shaved heads, sometimes with a plaited lock on one side.

Wigs

Comb

Hair pins

Comb

▲ Wigs were often long and elaborate and needed a lot of attention. Egyptians cared for their wigs with combs made of wood and ivory. They sometimes used curling tongs as well.

MAKE A MAGIC EYE CHARM

You will need

self-hardening modeling clay
length of leather strip or thick cord
pencil   poster paints
paintbrush   varnish

Knead the clay until soft and then shape into a wadjat eye. Add extra clay for the pupil of the eye and at the top of the charm. Use the pencil to make the top piece into a loop.

Leave the clay to harden. Paint in bright colors and leave to dry. Varnish. Thread the leather strip or cord through the loop and wear your charm for extra luck.

71

Sandals were made from papyrus and other reeds. Rich people, courtiers, and kings and queens wore padded leather ones. Footwear was a luxury item, and most ordinary people walked around barefoot. Colorful pictures of sandals were even painted onto the feet of mummies!

▼ Leather sandals.

▼ Reed sandals.

Baking and brewing

72 Bread was the most important food in the diet of ancient Egypt. Harvested grain was stored in huge granaries until needed. The Egyptians' favorite drink was beer. It was very thick and had to be strained before drinking. Models of brewers were even left in tombs to make sure the dead person had a plentiful supply of beer in the next world!

▼ An Egyptian banquet was a real occasion! Rich people could afford the best food and drink, but they would also have servants, as well as musicians and dancers.

73 A rough kind of bread was baked from either wheat or barley. The bread often contained gritty pieces that wore down the teeth of the Egyptians. Historians have discovered this by studying the teeth of mummies.

DESIGN A BANQUET MENU

A huge choice of foods was served at banquets for wealthy Egyptians. Meats such as duck, goose, gazelle, and heron, fresh fruits and vegetables, sweet pastries and cakes, with lots of beer and grape or date wine to drink.

Choose the foods for a banquet and design a decorative menu for your guests.

Hard day's work

74 Scribes were very important people in ancient Egypt. These highly skilled men kept records of everything that happened from day to day. They recorded all the materials used for building work, the numbers of cattle, and the crops that had been gathered for the royal family, the government, and the temples.

◀ Only the sons of scribes could undergo the strict scribe training, which began as early as the age of nine.

75 The libraries of ancient Egypt held thousands of papyrus scrolls. They covered subjects such as astronomy, medicine, geography, and law. Most ordinary Egyptians could not read or write, so the libraries were used only by educated people such as scribes and doctors.

76 Imagine if there were 700 letters in the alphabet! That was how many hieroglyphs Egyptian schoolchildren had to learn! Hieroglyphs were symbols that the Egyptians used for writing. Some symbols stood for words and some for sounds. Children went to schools for scribes where they first learned how to read and write hieroglyphs.

▼ Craftworkers produced statues and furniture for the pharoah. Workers such as these often had their own areas within a town. The village of Deir el-Medina was built specially for those who worked on tombs in the Valley of the Kings.

77 Most people worked as craftworkers or farm laborers. Craftworkers included carpenters, potters, weavers, jewelers, shoemakers, glassblowers, and perfume makers. Many sold their goods from small shops in the towns. They were kept busy making items for the pharaoh and wealthy people.

78 A typical lunch for a worker consisted of bread and onions. They may also have had a cucumber, washed down with a drink of beer.

QUIZ 4

Can you name the following items from life in ancient Egypt?

1.

2.

3.

4.

1. The dwarf god Bes 2. A canopic jar 3. A hair comb 4. An amulet

79 The base of the Great Pyramid takes up almost as much space as five football fields! Huge quantities of stone were needed to build these monuments. The Egyptians quarried limestone, sandstone, and granite for their buildings. In the surrounding desert they mined gold for decorations.

80 Slaves were often prisoners who had been captured from Egypt's enemies. They also came from the neighboring countries of Kush and Nubia. Life as a slave was not all bad. A slave could own land and buy goods—he could even buy his freedom!

Clever Egyptians

81 The insides of many Egyptian tombs were decorated with brightly colored wall paintings. They often depicted scenes from the dead person's life, showing him or her as a healthy young person. The Egyptians believed that these scenes would come to life in the next world.

sunken relief

▶ The Egyptians produced raised reliefs by cutting away the background, and sunken relief by cutting stone from inside the outline.

raised relief

82 Egyptian sculptors carved enormous stone statues of their pharaohs and gods. These were often placed outside a tomb or temple to guard the entrance. Scenes, called reliefs, were carved into the walls of temples and tombs. These often showed the person as they were when they were young, enjoying scenes from daily life. This was so that when the god Osiris brought the dead person and the tomb paintings back to life, the tomb owners would have a good time in the afterlife!

83 The ancient Egyptians had three different calendars: an everyday farming one, an astronomical, and a lunar (Moon) calendar. The 365-day farming calendar was made up of three seasons of four months. The astronomical calendar was based on observations of the star Sirius, which reappeared each year at the start of the flood season. Priests kept a calendar based on the movements of the Moon which told them when to perform ceremonies for to the moon god Khonsu.

▲ The days on this calendar are written in black and red. Black days are ordinary, but the red days are unlucky.

◄ Several artists worked on the tomb paintings. A junior artist drew the outlines of the scene, which were then checked and corrected by a more senior artist. Next, painters filled in the outlines in color.

84 Astronomers recorded their observations of the night skies. The Egyptian calendar was based on the movement of Sirius, the brightest star in the sky. The Egyptians used their knowledge of astronomy to build temples which lined up with certain stars or with the movement of the Sun.

I DON'T BELIEVE IT!

Bulbs of garlic were used to ward off snakes and to get rid of tapeworms from people's bodies.

85 Egyptian doctors knew how to set broken bones and treat illnesses such as fevers. They used medicines made from plants such as garlic and juniper to treat sick people. The Egyptians had a good knowledge of the basic workings of the human body.

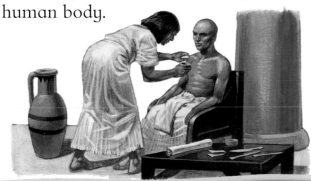

86 The Egyptians used a device called a nilometer to measure the depth of the river Nile. They inserted measuring posts into the riverbed at intervals along the bank so they could check the water levels at the start of each flood season.

From pictures to words

87 **The Egyptians had no paper—they wrote on papyrus.** It was made from the tall papyrus reeds that grew on the banks of the Nile. At first papyrus was sold as long strips, or scrolls, tied with string. Later the Egyptians put the papyrus sheets into books. Papyrus is very long lasting; sheets of papyrus have survived 3,000 years to the present day.

88 **Ink was made by mixing water with soot, charcoal, or colored minerals.** Scribes wrote in ink on papyrus scrolls, using reed brushes with specially shaped ends.

1. Papyrus was expensive because it took a long time to make. First people had to cut down the papyrus stems, and cut them up into lots of thin strips.

2. Then someone laid these strips in rows on a frame to form layers.

3. The papyrus strips were then pressed under weights. This squeezed out the water and squashed the layers together.

4. Finally, when the papyrus was dry, a man with a stone rubbed the surface smooth for writing.

89

The Rosetta Stone was found in 1799 by a French soldier in Egypt. It is a large slab of stone onto which three different kinds of writing have been carved: hieroglyphics, a simpler form of hieroglyphics called demotic, and Greek. All three sets of writing give an account of the coronation of King Ptolemy V. By translating the Greek, scholars could understand the Egyptian writing for the first time.

90

The ancient Egyptians used a system of picture writing called hieroglyphics. Each hieroglyph represented an object or a sound. For example, the picture of a lion represented the sound "l"; a basket represented the word "lord." Altogether there were about 700 different hieroglyphs. Scribes wrote them on papyrus scrolls or carved them into stone.

91

In the 5th century BC a Greek historian named Herodotus wrote about life in ancient Egypt. As he traveled across the country he observed and wrote about people's daily lives, and their religion and customs such as embalming and mummification—he even wrote about cats!

WRITE YOUR NAME IN HIEROGLYPHICS

Below you will see the hieroglyphic alphabet. I have written my name in hieroglyphs. Can you write yours?

J A N E

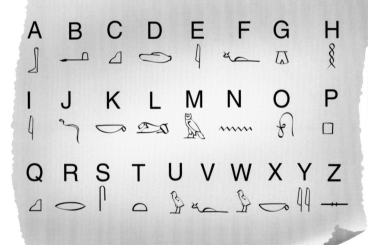

92

The hieroglyphs of a ruler's name were written inside an oval-shaped frame called a cartouche. The pharaoh's cartouche was carved on pillars and temple walls, painted on tomb walls and mummy cases, and written on official documents.

Fun and games

93 Hippo hunting was a dangerous but popular sport in ancient Egypt. Hunters in reed boats, armed only with spears and ropes, killed hippos in the waters of the Nile. In the desert, hunters chased lions, antelope, wild bulls, gazelles, and hares. Marsh birds were killed with throwing sticks that were like boomerangs.

▲ Hunting was reserved mostly for royalty and courtiers. Amenhotep III was said to have killed more than 100 lions in 10 years.

MAKE A SNAKE GAME

You will need

sheet of thick cardboard
large dinner plate   paintbrush
scissors   colored pens
white paint   counters
pencil   two dice

Place the plate on the cardboard and draw round the outside. Cut out the circle. Paint one side with paint. Leave to dry.

Draw a snake's head in the center of the board. Draw small circles (about 1in (2cm) across) spreading out from the center until you reach the edge of the board. Color the circles to make an attractive pattern.

Place a counter for each player on the outside square. The winner is the first player to reach the snake's head.

94 The Egyptians played various board games, a few of which we still play today. The game of senet was supposed to represent the struggle between good and evil on the journey into the next world. Players moved sets of counters across the board according to how their throwing sticks (like modern dice) landed. Another popular board game was called hounds and jackals.

Heroes and heroines

95 **Ramses II built more temples than any other Egyptian ruler.** Two of his greatest achievements are the huge rock-cut temple at Abu Simbel and the Great Hall at Karnak. He also finished building the mortuary temple of Seti I at Luxor. After his death a further nine pharaohs were given the name Ramses.

Lapis lazuli is a bright-blue semiprecious gem that the Egyptians used to decorate the coffins of rich people

▼ The Great Hall at Karnak.

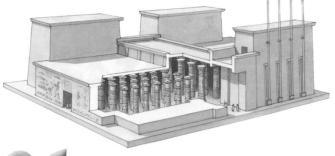

96 **Queen Hatshepsut was often depicted wearing men's clothing and a false beard.** She was the wife of Thutmose II. On his death Hatshepsut took the title of pharaoh and adopted the royal symbols of the double crown, the crook, the flail (whip)—and also the ceremonial beard!

▶ During her 20-year reign Hatshepsut sent an expedition of five ships to Punt on the coast of the Red Sea. The ships brought back incense, copper, and ivory.

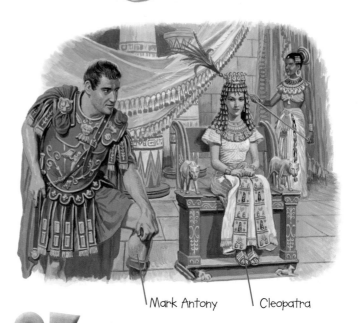

Mark Antony   Cleopatra

97 **Queen Cleopatra VII was one of the last rulers of ancient Egypt.** She fell in love with the Roman emperor Julius Caesar, and later married the Roman general Mark Antony. Cleopatra killed herself in 30BC when the Romans conquered Egypt.

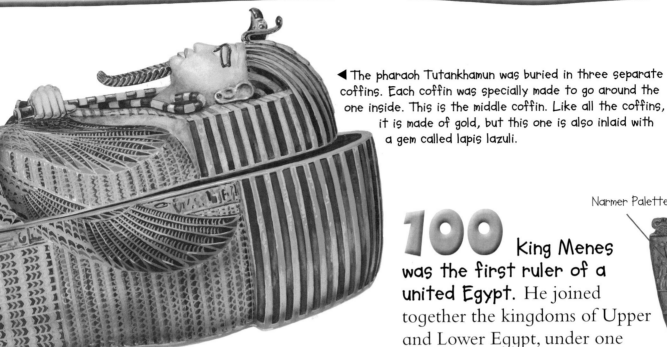

◄ The pharaoh Tutankhamun was buried in three separate coffins. Each coffin was specially made to go around the one inside. This is the middle coffin. Like all the coffins, it is made of gold, but this one is also inlaid with a gem called lapis lazuli.

Narmer Palette

100 King Menes was the first ruler of a united Egypt.
He joined together the kingdoms of Upper and Lower Egypt, under one government, in around 3100BC. Menes was also called Narmer. Archaeologists have found a slate tablet, called the Narmer Palette, that shows him beating his enemies in battle.

98 Tutankhamun is probably the most famous pharaoh of all.
His tomb, with its fabulous treasure of over 5,000 objects, was discovered complete in 1922. Tutankhamun was only nine years old when he became ruler, and he died at the young age of about 17. He was buried in the Valley of the Kings.

99 Thutmose III was a clever general who added new lands to ancient Egypt.
Under his leadership, Egypt's armies seized territory in Syria to the north and Palestine to the east. During his reign Thutmose ordered a giant obelisk made of granite to be placed at Heliopolis—it now stands on the bank of the river Thames in London.

QUIZ 5

1. Name two popular drinks in ancient Egypt.

2. What is a cartouche?

3. What is the Rosetta Stone?

4. What is senet?

5. Explain why Queen Hatshepsut was unusual.

1. Beer and wine 2. An oval plaque on which the pharaoh's name was written. 3. The stone that enabled historians to read hieroglyphs. 4. An ancient Egyptian game. 5. She ruled as a pharaoh, wearing the ceremonial beard.